WRONGFUL CONVICTIONS

True Murder Cases
Unbelievable Miscarriages of Justice

Jack Smith

DISCLAIMER

All rights reserved. No part of this publication or the information in it may be quoted from or reproduced in any form by means such as printing, scanning, photocopying, or otherwise without prior written permission of the copyright holder.

Disclaimer and Terms of Use: Effort has been made to ensure that the information in this book is accurate and complete. However, the author and the publisher do not warrant the accuracy of the information, text, and graphics contained within the book due to the rapidly changing nature of science, research, known and unknown facts, and internet. The author and the publisher do not hold any responsibility for errors, omissions, or contrary interpretation of the subject matter herein. This book is presented solely for motivational and informational purposes only.

CONTENTS

DISCLAIMER _____ 3

INTRODUCTION _____ 1

ELIZA FENNING _____ 5

THE MESSALINA OF ILFORD _____ 39

"LET HIM HAVE IT"- THE TRAGEDY OF DEREK BENTLEY ___ 63

CONCLUSION _____ 81

EXCERPTS FROM JACK SMITH'S BOOK SERIAL KILLERS
EXPLORING THE HORRIFIC CRIMES OF LITTLE KNOWN
MURDERERS _____ 83

OTHER BOOKS FROM JACK SMITH _____ 97

SOURCES _____ 98

INTRODUCTION

Ever since DNA evidence started exonerating death row inmates, public concern about wrongful executions has been on the rise. It has been such a source of worry that some states have abolished the death penalty entirely.

When Governor Pat Quinn made Illinois the 16th state to stop using capital punishment in March 2011, he stated, "Since our experience has shown that there is no way to design a perfect death penalty system, free from the numerous flaws that can lead to wrongful convictions or discriminatory treatment, I have concluded that the proper course of action is to abolish it."

Although we want to believe that the criminal justice system designed to protect us is infallible, mistakes can be and are made. The ultimate tragedy is when an innocent person is executed for a crime that he or she didn't commit.

This volume revisits three tragic stories of wrongful executions in the UK, where justice was swift and limitless appeals were not supported. In one case the person was actually exonerated forty-six years after being hanged.

- **Eliza Fenning and the Devilish Dumplings:** In March 1815, the entire household of Robert Turner, a London law stationer, was struck by a mysterious illness. When a search was made for its cause, a substance believed to be arsenic was found in the dish used to mix up yeast dumplings the family had eaten for dinner. Although she had fallen ill too, Eliza Fenning, the twenty-one-year-old maid who had prepared the dumplings, was charged with attempted murder and hanged. Her execution is still regarded as one of Britain's worst miscarriages of justice.

- **The Messalina of Ilford:** Edith Thompson and her younger lover, Frederick Bywaters, were executed in January 1923 for the murder of Edith's husband. Although Mr. Bywaters confessed and insisted that Mrs. Thompson had nothing to do with the murder, she was held equally responsible for the crime because of some letters that expressed hostile intent toward her overbearing spouse. Her supporters believed that she had really been condemned for being an adulteress. There is currently a campaign in process to win her a posthumous royal pardon.

- **"Let Him Have It":** On January 28, 1953, nineteen-year-old Derek Bentley was hanged at Wandsworth Prison for the murder of a Metropolitan Police constable. Bentley had not fired the fatal shot, but his sixteen-year-old accomplice was too young to receive the death penalty, so the mentally impaired Bentley went to the gallows instead. In 1998, thanks to four decades of vigorous campaigning by his family, he received a posthumous pardon. His execution was instrumental in the abolition of capital punishment in the UK.

It is too late to save these victims of wrongful execution, but the time has come to accept that, regardless of our individual feelings about the death penalty, all future debates on the subject must proceed with the knowledge that innocent people have been put to death.

ELIZA FENNING

Eliza Fenning at the time of her trial (Author's collection)

On March 21, 1815, a sudden and mysterious illness struck the household of Robert Turner at 68 Chancery

Lane in London. The event resulted in only one death, however, and that death took place four months later, on the scaffold at Newgate.

Turner, a law stationer[1], his wife Charlotte, and father Orlebar (who was his partner in the business) were enjoying a hearty meal of steak, potatoes, and yeast dumplings when Mrs. Turner suddenly stood up, complaining of feeling unwell, and went upstairs. A few minutes later she was violently ill. Robert and Orlebar Turner also began vomiting and complaining of severe stomach pains. So did Roger Gadsden, one of Robert's apprentices, and Eliza Fenning, the servant who had prepared the meal.

No one died, but most of the household was in agony for hours. When a search was made for the cause of the illness, what appeared to be arsenic was found in the dish used to mix up the dumplings.

Suspicion fell on 21-year-old Eliza Fenning, the cook and general maid who had been with the family since January. She was a hard worker but there had supposedly been some problems with her moral conduct

---

[1] Law stationers stocked and provided forms required by lawyers, such as court applications, licenses, etc.

in relation to some apprentices who also lived in the house.

Although the young servant had been as ill as everyone else that night, she was arrested and charged with intent to commit murder. At her trial the following April the Recorder of London[2] summed up the case in a way that was highly prejudicial to the defense. The jury found her guilty and she was sentenced to death.

In the months that followed Eliza Fenning protested her innocence, and many people believed her. They included eminent personages like Charles Dickens and Samuel Parr, a Doctor of Law and celebrated political writer. Her controversial conviction became a *cause célèbre* during the days leading up to her execution. Afterward, thousands of grieving supporters accompanied her coffin to the church grounds, convinced that a miscarriage of justice had taken place.

They were probably right.

Elizabeth Fenning, whom everyone called Eliza, was born on June 10, 1793, the daughter of hard-working but poor parents. She had one brother, who was killed in an

---

[2] Senior judge of London's Criminal Court

accident while still young, leaving her an only child. Although her father, William Fenning, had served with the British land forces during the Napoleonic Wars, and seen active duty in Martinique, Guadeloupe, and St. Lucia, his military pension was small, so Eliza went out to work at the age of fourteen, serving various households as a domestic servant.

In January 1815 she entered Robert Turner's home as cook and servant. The Turners had another maid, Sarah Peer, but Charlotte was five months pregnant and needed additional help with the meals and housework.

Two young men, Roger Gadsden and Thomas King, who were apprenticed to Orlebar and Robert Turner, also lived there. They were apparently one source of the discord that arose soon after Eliza's arrival: Charlotte Turner later testified that in late January or early February, she saw Eliza enter the young mens' room in a state of partial undress.

Neither the young woman nor the teenaged apprentices ever publicly explained what she had been doing. It's doubtful that her intentions were immoral, as there were no attempts to conceal her presence in the room. At the time, Eliza was actually engaged to be married[3]. But the following morning the scandalized mistress remonstrated with her servant and threatened her with dismissal. When Eliza was appropriately contrite Charlotte relented, but thought she detected a sullenness afterward.

During the first week in March, Eliza asked her mistress if she could make yeast dumplings, a dish she claimed to excel at. Charlotte declined: she preferred to make dumplings using dough from the baker. When the brewer brought some yeast on March 20, Mrs. Turner told Eliza the following day that she could make the dumplings, but gave precise directions on how the dough was to be mixed.

While Eliza was working in the kitchen, Charlotte went to see how the other servant, Sarah Peer, was making out with her own task: repairing a counterpane in the master bedroom window. She would later assert that no one but Eliza was in the kitchen while the dumpling dough was being made.

When Charlotte returned to check on the dough, which had been set in a pan before the fire to rise, she

---

[3] Her fiance was never named, and she protected his identity during the scandal that followed.

observed that it looked flat and 'singular'. She mentioned this to Eliza, but the young woman was unconcerned.

"It will rise before I want it (to make dinner)," she said.

At 3:00 p.m., Robert, Charlotte, and Orlebar Turner sat down to a dinner of rump steak, potatoes, and dumplings. When Sarah Peer brought the soon-to-be infamous dumplings from the kitchen, Charlotte commented to her that they looked strange: "black and heavy, instead of white and light."

Their appearance did not prevent her from serving some to her husband and father-in-law before eating a small piece herself, along with a few bites of beefsteak. Minutes later her stomach began to burn. When the pain increased, she excused herself and went to her bedroom, where she collapsed and began to vomit.

The two men continued to eat, unaware that Charlotte was seriously ill. Suddenly Robert Turner got up from the table and disappeared downstairs. When he failed to return immediately, his father rose too and went looking for him. Orlebar found Robert at the foot of the lower staircase, eyes swollen and face drenched in sweat. It was obvious that he had been vomiting.

"This is very extraordinary," the older man said, just before heat exploded in his stomach and chest. He barely made it out into the yard before throwing up his dinner.

Roger Gadsden, one of the apprentices, wandered into the kitchen around that time. He was unaware of the unfolding drama; like most servants and apprentices in 1815, he did not dine with his masters. At two o'clock he, Thomas King, and the two servants had eaten a simple beef steak pie that Eliza had prepared for their meal at Mrs. Turner's request.

Seeing what was left of the dumplings on the kitchen table, Gadsden moved to take one, but Eliza tried to dissuade him, saying that they were "cold and heavy" and would do him "no good."

He persisted in eating a small piece. Seeing that there was also leftover gravy, he dipped a piece of bread in it and enjoyed a snack. Then he went into Robert Turner's office to finish up some paperwork.

As Gadsden later recalled, at around 3:20 Turner came weakly out of the office and said he was very ill. Ten minutes later, the apprentice felt a burning pain in his own stomach, although it was not severe enough to make him vomit. When his master sent him to Lambeth by coach to fetch Margaret Turner, the latter's mother, Gadsden obeyed, but was in agony the entire time.

"I was very sick going and coming back," he remembered. "I thought I should die."

When Margaret Turner arrived, she found everyone in a dire state. Even Eliza was vomiting and on the verge of collapse; she admitted later that she'd tasted a piece of leftover dumpling after Gadsden seemed to relish his portion.

"Oh, those devilish dumplings," the older woman exclaimed. It is unclear how she knew that dumplings had been on the menu, unless Gadsden told her.

"Not the dumplings, but the milk, ma'am," Eliza groaned.

"Milk? What milk?"

"The milk that Sally (Sarah) fetched to make the sauce (gravy)."

A surgeon named Ogilvy, whose practice was also on Chancery Lane, was summoned at around five o'clock.

He gave everyone a full dose of castor oil to purge the irritants from their systems and also administered doses of milk, water, and sugar, which were contemporary remedies for nausea and dehydration.

When the mass illness failed to abate and Ogilvy started showing signs of exhaustion, Thomas King (the other apprentice) was sent to the Piccadilly home of John Marshall, a member of the Royal College of Surgeons and apothecary to the Duke of Gloucester. The frightened young man stammered that the entire household was in a deplorable state, and most of its members might die before the doctor could see them.

Shortly after nine, Marshall, who had known the Turner family for years, arrived to find Eliza lying on the stairs, moaning and retching. She told him that she had been vomiting non-stop, her head ached, and she was desperately thirsty. After directing her to drink some milk and water, Marshall went upstairs and found the Turners in bed.

Robert complained of excruciating stomach and abdominal pain. His extremities were cold, light hurt his eyes, and like Fenning, his head ached and an unquenchable thirst tormented him. When he attempted to get out of bed to take something off the night table, Turner suddenly collapsed to the floor in what the doctor called an "epileptic fit" and took a while to revive. Charlotte was in similar shape, making Marshall fear a possible miscarriage.

With help from Margaret Turner and Dr. Ogilvy, Marshall worked to stabilize everyone. When the two medical men went to the garret bedroom to treat Eliza, she turned away from them.

"I won't take anything," she said. "I'd much rather die than live: life is no consequence to me."

Marshall and Ogilvy were surprised but insisted on her taking the milk mixture and purgatives that had been given to everyone else. She reluctantly told the men to leave the remedies on her night table, but never took them.

Eliza Fenning's detractors (which included Dr. Marshall, who published a pamphlet that 'proved' her guilt) would hold up this incident as proof that she was intent on murder-suicide. That is one possibility. The likelier explanation is that Eliza knew that if the Turners succumbed, her chances of working again were very poor. Who would hire a cook if her employers died after eating a meal she prepared? She preferred death to a painful, poverty-ridden future.

When Marshall felt that it was safe to do so, he and his colleague went home for some rest, returning the following morning to find the household still sick but slowly rallying. With the crisis passing, it was time to determine what exactly had happened.

******

Mr. Turner senior suspected they had been poisoned, as a packet of arsenic kept in Robert Turner's desk drawer to deal with mice had gone missing around two weeks before. Having recovered sufficiently to start investigating, he entered the kitchen and inspected the pots and pans, which had not yet been washed and put away.

Finding the brown dish that the dumplings had been mixed in, he put some water in it, stirred, and noticed that a white powder sank to the bottom. It was a common misconception of the day that utensils that had come into contact with a deadly substance would turn black. To confirm his suspicion, he retrieved those that had been used to serve the dumplings. They were black.[4]

Turner sought out Dr. Marshall and asked him to examine the white substance. The surgeon washed the mixing dish with a kettle of warm water and observed the powdery material that sank to the bottom. He concluded that it was arsenic.

In 1815 only three tests existed for detecting arsenic, none of them foolproof. Toxicology had yet to be developed into an exact science, and Marshall was not one of the acknowledged experts. However, he was able to convince Orlebar Turner, who went to Eliza Fenning's garret bedroom and demanded to know how such a toxic ingredient could have found its way into the dumplings. She responded that it must have been in the milk that Sarah Peer had brought in.

Suspicion mounted against Eliza. She had made the dumplings, and by her own admission, no one else had been in the kitchen at that time.

Turner decided to get the authorities involved. Accompanied by Dr. Marshall, he went to the Hatton Garden Police Court, returning soon afterward with a policeman named William Thisselton. They found the

---

[4] It was believed that if silver utensils came into contact with a deadly substance such as arsenic or cyanide, they would turn black. This is not the case, although extended contact with garlic or onion, which release hydrogen sulfide, can cause silver to change color.

young woman out of bed and fully dressed, making them suspect that she intended to flee.

Relations between servants and their masters or mistresses were not always harmonious, which is hardly surprising despite the firm class system in place in Georgian England. Young people sometimes rebelled against the employers and masters who had authority over them, and London courts often heard cases involving servants accused of theft and masters charged with refusing to pay wages.

Although uncommon, murderous servants were not unheard of. During the French Revolution, scores of them had risen up and butchered their former superiors, and since then many a master or mistress had regarded disgruntled employees with hostility and fear. This was certainly the case with Eliza Fenning; Charlotte Turner publicly wondered if the reprimand in January caused a murder attempt in March.

William Thisselton asked Eliza if there could have been something wrong with the flour. She denied it, saying that she had used the same flour to make crust for the beef steak pie that the servants ate for dinner that day.

She said she thought the yeast might be to blame, as she'd seen red sediment in its container afterward.

The men exchanged glances. First, Eliza had blamed the milk. Now it was the yeast?
This wavering would be held up as additional proof of guilt. No one seems to have considered that Eliza herself was trying to understand how this could have happened. The milk and the yeast were the only meal ingredients that had been newly obtained on the day in question. She was considering both possible causes, certain the problem must have originated with one or the other.

After being allowed to collect her belongings in a box, Fenning was taken to Hatton Garden Police Court on March 23, charged with administering arsenic to the Turner family with intent to murder them, and committed for trial.
Dr. Marshall, who published an anti-Fenning pamphlet in late 1815, claimed that when her box of possessions was searched at the prison, an 'infamous book' that contained abortion instructions was found. He followed up this detail with the comment, "She having been frequently heard in the kitchen to say 'She would have her spite out with her mistress', further illustrates the

idea of premeditated revenge, and shows the depravity of her morals."

Although illegal, books that contained abortion advice were not as unusual in 1815 as Dr. Marshall liked to believe. Young female servants were regular targets of unwanted male attention, thanks to their relative powerlessness in Georgian era households, and pregnancy would typically be followed by job loss and social disgrace. For these women, such books were a necessary evil, and one they took pains to hide lest they encounter reactions like Dr. Marshall's.

As for her spiteful comments, Eliza Fenning was not the first servant to be resentful over a reprimand. Presumably this report came from Sarah Peer, who would testify against her at the trial. Strangely, the statement that Marshall attributed to Eliza about having "her spite out" with Charlotte Turner was never part of the official record.

******

On April 11, 1815, the case was heard before Sir John Silvester, Recorder of the City of London, at the Old Bailey, London's criminal courthouse.

In retrospect, Eliza Fenning was unfortunate to appear before Silvester. Prior to his appointment as Recorder of London, he had been Common Serjeant, which was the second most senior judge of the Criminal Court. While occupying this post, he was widely regarded as 'uncouth and overly severe'.[5]

Charlotte Turner testified first. She confirmed the date that Eliza came to work for the Turners and recounted the incident involving the nocturnal visit to the apprentices, adding that the young woman had been moody toward her afterward. After establishing a potential motive for attempted murder, Mrs. Turner recalled how Eliza had been practically begging to make yeast dumplings since the beginning of March, when the arsenic disappeared from Robert Turner's desk.

After eating less than a quarter of a dumpling, she said, she "felt an extreme burning pain in her stomach, which increased every minute."

Orlebar Turner recounted his own ordeal. When asked if his nausea was of the "common kind" one might

---

[5] May, Allyson N. *The Bar & The Old Bailey (1750-1850)* p. 150

experience with a stomach flu, he replied, "I never experienced anything like it before for violence."

"Did the prisoner give you any assistance while you were sick?"

"None in the least."

The question—and its answer—gave the jury the impression that Eliza had been callously indifferent to everyone's suffering. They had not yet heard about her own bout with the same symptoms.

The elder Mr. Turner confirmed that he had kept a packet of arsenic in the office desk drawer to deal with mice. It had been labelled, 'Arsenic, deadly poison'.

"Do you happen to know whether the prisoner can read?" Sir Silvester asked.

"I believe she can read and write."

Silvester looked at Mrs. Turner. "Is that so?"

"She can read and write very well," Charlotte nodded.

Once again the jury received a clear message: Eliza could read, so she would have known upon seeing the packet that it contained poison. When Turner added that Eliza regularly opened that desk drawer to get waste paper to light the office fire, the implication was impossible to miss.

Turner was followed to the stand by his wife Margaret, Roger Gadsden, and Robert Turner. The latter made a statement that contradicted what Eliza told Margaret Turner about the milk in the sauce being to blame.

Q. *Did you partake of the dumplings?*

A. *Yes, I did.*

Q. *Did you eat any of the sauce?*

A. *Not a portion of it whatever.*

Sarah Peer, the other servant, testified that after Charlotte had reprimanded Eliza for her inappropriate conduct with the apprentices, the young woman had grumbled that she "should not like Mr. and Mrs. Robert Turner."

William Thisselton, the police official who arrested Eliza, recounted her statement about having seen red sediment in the yeast. Joseph Parson, servant to the brewer, said that he often brought beer to the Turner household. He added that the Thursday before the mishap, Eliza asked him for some yeast, which he delivered the following Monday.

John Marshall, the second doctor to come, recounted his hurried visit to the stricken household. "The symptoms were such as would be produced by arsenic," he said.

Q. Will arsenic, cut with a knife, will it produce on the knife the color of blackness?

A. I have no doubt of it. I examined the remains of the yeast. There was no arsenic in that.

The symptoms may have mirrored arsenic poisoning, but arsenic could not have turned the silverware black. As apothecary to the Duke of Gloucester, however, Marshall was considered above reproach.

Eliza Fenning's counsel, a Mr. Alley, called four character witnesses. One of them, a Mr. Smyth, told the court that he had encountered Eliza two days before the catastrophe and she had seemed cheerful, telling him that she was comfortable in her situation with the Turners. The other witnesses told similar stories.

When it was her turn to speak, Eliza said, "My lord, I am truly innocent of all the charges, as God is my witness. I am innocent, indeed I am. I liked my place, I was very comfortable. As to my master saying I did not assist him, I was too ill. I had no concern with the drawer at all; when I wanted a piece of paper (to light the fire) I always asked for it."

Sir Silvester summed up to the jury as follows:

Gentlemen, you have now heard the evidence given on this trial, and the case lies in a very narrow compass. There are but two questions for your consideration, and these are, whether poison was administered, in all, to four persons, and by what hand such poison was given. That these persons were poisoned appears certain from the evidence of Mrs Charlotte Turner, Haldebart (sic) Turner, Roger Gadsden, the apprentice, and Robert Turner; for each of these persons ate of the dumplings, and were all more or less affected—that is, they were everyone poisoned.

That the poison was in the dough of which these dumplings were composed has been fully proved, I think, by the testimony of the surgeon who examined the remains of the dough left in the dish in which the dumplings had been mixed and divided; and he deposes that the powder which had subsided at the bottom of the dish was arsenic.

That the arsenic was not in the flour I think appears plain, from the circumstance that the crust of a pie had been made that very morning with some of the same flour of which the dumplings were made and the persons who dined off the pie felt no inconvenience whatever; that it was not in the yeast nor in the milk has been also proved; neither could it be in the sauce, for two of the persons who were ill never touched a particle of the sauce, and yet were violently affected with retching and sickness.

From all these circumstances it must follow that the poisonous ingredient was in the dough alone; for, besides that the persons who partook of the dumplings at dinner were all more or less affected by what they had eaten, it was observed by one of the witnesses that the dough retained the same shape it had when first put into the dish to rise, and that it appeared dark, and was heavy, and in fact never did rise.

The other question for your consideration is, by what hand the poison was administered; and although we have nothing before us but circumstantial evidence, yet it often happens that circumstances are more conclusive than the most positive testimony. The prisoner, when taxed with poisoning the dumplings, threw the blame first on the milk, next on the yeast, and then on the sauce; but it has been proved, most satisfactorily, that none of these contained it, and that it was in the dumplings alone, which no person but the prisoner had made.

Gentlemen, if poison had been given even to a dog, one would suppose that common humanity would have prompted us to assist it in its agonies: here is the case of a master and a mistress being both poisoned, and no assistance was offered. Gentlemen, I have now stated all the facts as they have arisen, and I leave the case in your hands, being fully persuaded that, whatever your verdict may be, you will conscientiously discharge your duty both to your God and to your country."

After a few minutes' deliberation the jury returned a verdict of guilty. When Silvester sentenced her to hang, Eliza collapsed. One reporter present in the court noted, "She was carried from the dock convulsed with agony and uttering frightful screams."

The verdict and its harsh sentence aroused considerable public disquiet. Radical journalist and publisher William Hone ranted against the trial's outcome in his weekly newspaper, *The Traveller*, and letters flooded the London newspaper offices, many of them taking issue with the evidence against the unfortunate girl. One person wrote:

I have been informed, sir, and I believe the information to have been founded on fact, that a professional man has had arsenic mixed in dumplings for experiment, and they rose as customary, were neither black nor heavy, nor did they particularly colour the knives.

Another individual, whose letter was published in the *Examiner* on May 14, stated, "It has been observed by many gentlemen that if they had been on the jury of Elizabeth Fenning, they could not have found her guilty, because there was no proof that she was the actual person who put the poison in the pan, knowing it to be poison."

The *Examiner* editor, commenting on this letter, wrote:
The observations of our Correspondent prove nothing; but still many persons are of opinion that the guilt of this young woman has not been sufficiently shewn (sic). The

arsenic, it appeared, was kept in an open drawer with waste paper, to which everyone might resort. This was a negligent practice, to say the very least.

One correspondent summed it up perfectly:

I have never read or heard of a case equally wicked in one light, and foolish in the other—wicked in the extreme, for contriving to take away the lives of those who had never offended her—insane, by taking such a degree of the bane, as subjected herself to as great a degree of affliction as any one of the family. Far from being wickedly cunning does she appear to me, as it is evident she left the pan in which the dumplings were made unwashed until the next day; nor did she attempt to put the remainder of the dumplings out of the way; the doing of which the perpetrator of such a crime would not have omitted.

Simply put, Eliza Fenning had no conceivable reason for annihilating the Turner family. The occasional disagreement aside, she was apparently happy in her position. Writing to the British press in May 1815, a man named F.M. Barran pointed out that she was "not such a one as my Lord or my Lady would have either for a housemaid or cook: a place of all work was, therefore, the situation of this little female previous to going into Mr. Turner's family, which made her feel perfectly contented with her late situation."

Translated, this mean that although cheerful and hardworking, she had been too young and common to obtain a privileged position in an upper-class household, so the Turner position was a stroke of good luck. She may have been grumpy toward Charlotte after being scolded, but that was hardly a murderous reaction, and she could just as easily have quit if she found the situation unbearable. Murder was an option only an insane person would have considered, and Eliza Fenning had shown no signs of mental derangement.

The morning of Wednesday, July 26 was set for her execution. In the interim, various appeals were made for clemency to the Prince Regent, the Home Secretary and the Lord Chancellor. The week before the hanging was scheduled to take place, the Home Office considered her case.

Lord Sidmouth, the Home Secretary who normally made clemency decisions, was away, but Lord Eldon (the Lord Chancellor) met with the Recorder, Sir John Silvester. After conferring with Silvester and interviewing witnesses

(Roger Gadsden was summoned from the spa in Bath where he had been sent to recover), they decided that there were no grounds to interfere with the course of justice. Given the popular opinion about Fenning's innocence, Lord Eldon was uneasy enough to call a second meeting in the evening, but its result was the same.

There was no more hope.

Eliza received the devastating news stoically enough, but from time to time terror broke through her composure. The Sunday before the scheduled execution, she received the sacrament and heard the 'condemned sermon'. Overcome by the intensity of her feelings, she became hysterical and could not be calmed until evening.

The following day, Monday, July 24, Eliza wrote a letter to the Turners, asking them to come and see her. When they complied, she asserted that she had not attempted to poison them and hoped that one day the true culprit would come to light.

She saw her mother for the last time on Tuesday evening. When they prepared to finally part, she said earnestly, "Now, my dear mother, I embrace you for the last time, and with this embrace, receive the only consolation I can give you, and that is a solemn and a sincere declaration of my innocence of the horrid crime for which I am to suffer."

A lot of people believed her. That night, an angry crowd assembled outside the Turner home at 68 Chancery Lane and threatened to pull it down. Only the timely arrival of the police prevented them from exacting their vengeance.

******

Eliza Fenning slept well, and spent the last morning of her life writing letters. While she worked by candlelight, the large portable gallows was taken out of storage and assembled outside the Debtor's Door section of Newgate. A triple hanging, the only one of its kind in 1815, was on the agenda: Eliza would hang along with 24-year-old William Oldfield, who had raped a nine-year-old girl, and 51-year-old Abraham Adams, who had been found guilty of sodomy.

Shortly before dawn people began to assemble in the streets outside the prison, eager for a good position from which to watch the executions, which were scheduled for

8:00 a.m. These crowds were known for their rowdiness, and this one was no exception—at first. But when Eliza Fenning appeared shortly before eight, everyone fell silent.

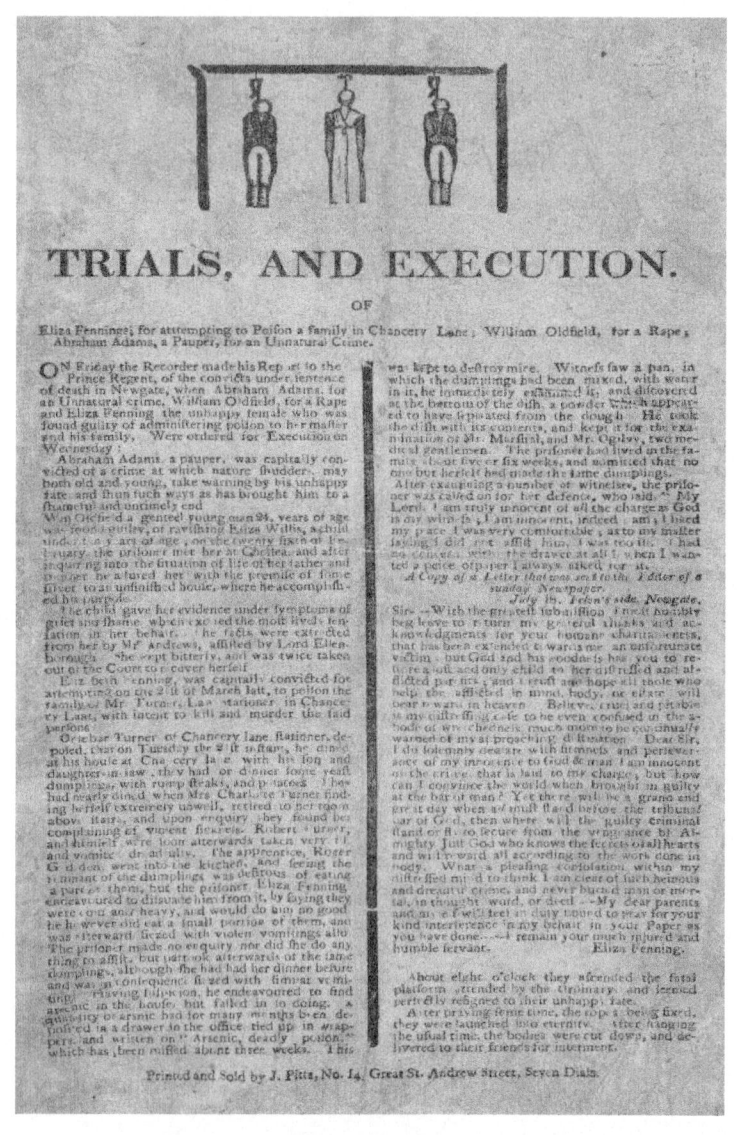

Broadsheet published after the triple hanging
(Author's collection)

She presented a slender, attractive figure in her high-waisted muslin gown and cap and high-laced lilac boots. Oldfield, the rapist, approached her and urged her to pray, saying that when it was over they should all be happy. Eliza said nothing as the sheriff's officers pinioned her arms.

Reverend Horace Cotton, the Ordinary of Newgate, accompanied her as she ascended the scaffold. When asked if she had anything to communicate in these final moments, Eliza replied, "Before the just and Almighty God, and by the faith of the Holy Sacrament I have taken, I am innocent of the offence with which I am charged."

She stood calmly while the hangman, John Langley, tried to draw the traditional white cotton cap over her head. Her muslin cap was too large to allow it, so Langley attempt to bind a handkerchief over her face instead, but the piece of fabric was too small. As a last resort, he took out his own pocket handkerchief.

Eliza recoiled in disgust, as the cloth was not clean. Turning to Reverend Cotton, she implored, "Pray do not let him put it on, Mr. Cotton. Pray make him take it off. Pray do!"

"My dear, it must be on," Cotton replied. "He must put it on."

She stopped resisting and let the hangman tie the dirty handkerchief over her face before placing the noose around her neck.

When the preparations were complete, Langley released the pin holding the trap in place and the three condemned prisoners fell about 18 inches. This 'short' drop method of hanging more often than not resulted in a slow death by strangulation, but by all accounts Eliza died without a struggle. She twitched once before going still, much to the relief of the spectators who felt she had suffered enough over the preceding months.

William and Mary Fenning had to pay the 14s. 6d. 'executioner fee' before they could claim their daughter's body for burial. She was put on display on an open coffin for three days at their home so that the public could pay its respects, and many people came. The summer heat had little effect on her appearance. According to one report, she was 'seemingly in a sweet sleep, with a smile on her countenance.'

The funeral started at 3:30 p.m. at the Fenning home in Eagle Street, Red Lion Square on July 31. The procession to the graveyard of St. George the Martyr consisted of her parents and six chief mourners, the undertaker, six young women dressed in white, and a bevy of peace officers who were there to prevent any demonstrations. Thousands of silent Londoners followed and watched from rooftops and windows. It was later estimated that over ten thousand people assembled in and about the churchyard.

Eliza Fenning was dead and buried, but she was not destined to be forgotten.

******

Charles Dickens was only three years old when Eliza Fenning died, but learned of her story decades later, when he was editor of *All the Year Round*, a weekly journal. Writing to a friend in October 1867 he stated, "I told you some time ago that I believed the arsenic in Eliza Fenning's case to have been administered by the apprentice. I was never more convinced of anything in my life than in that girl's innocence."[6] He never specified which apprentice he was referring to, but said that the

---

[6] Dickens, Charles, and Georgina Hogarth. *The Letters of Charles Dickens*, p. 240

youth in question was known to have made poison threats against the Turners.[7]

William Hone, the publisher and satirist who had tirelessly advocated for Eliza in *The Traveller*, turned his energies toward a posthumous exoneration. He wrote a book that must now be considered a landmark in investigative journalism: *The Important Results of an Elaborate Investigation into the Mysterious Case of Eliza Fenning*. It demolished the prosecution's case against her and revealed facts that did not make it into the trial transcript, such as Eliza's complaints to her mistress that Roger Gadsden had behaved 'improperly' toward her and that she had gone into the apprentice's room that night to remove the candle that they had left burning.

A druggist named Gibson had an interesting story to tell Hone. He said that in September or October 1814, Robert Turner had come to his home, behaving erratically. Gibson was so concerned that he invited Turner into a back room and detained him while a colleague summoned Orlebar Turner.

---

[7] It is not known what became of Thomas King, but Roger Gadsden was admitted to the bar after completing his apprenticeship and became a founding partner of the firm Gadsden and Flower.

During the ensuing wait, Robert uttered exclamations such as "My dear Gibson, do, for God's sake, get me secured or confined, for if I am at liberty I shall do some mischief. I shall destroy myself and my wife! I must and shall do it, unless all means of destruction are removed out of my way. Therefore do, my good friend, have me put under some kind of restraint! Something from above tells me that I must do it, and unless I am prevented, I certainly shall do it."

When Orlebar Turner arrived, Gibson urged him to do something about his deranged son. Turner admitted that other friends had, as the druggist recalled it, "mentioned the impropriety of Mr. Robert G. Turner's being at large under the circumstances with which he was afflicted."

Gibson swore that he had made this information available to Sir John Silvester prior to Eliza Fenning's execution, but it was not acted upon.

Robert Turner certainly knew about the arsenic in the office drawer. Could he have stolen it while in a melancholy state and used it two weeks later to try to annihilate his family? Although Charlotte Turner insisted that Eliza had never left the dumpling dough alone, the young woman had in fact left the kitchen briefly to accept a coal delivery. The dough could easily have been tainted during that time.

After the Regency period ended, Eliza Fenning continued to be remembered by the Victorians, especially those who were firmly against capital punishment. Even today, her execution is held up as an example of a system whose mistakes are irreversible.

THE MESSALINA OF ILFORD

January 9, 1923

John Ellis had been England's Chief Executioner since 1907, and took his position seriously. Unlike many of his predecessors, who were not opposed to 'botching' a hanging to give the crowds a good show when public executions were legal, Ellis concentrated on dispatching condemned criminals as quickly and painlessly as possible.

During his career he had executed many of the country's most infamous killers: Dr. Hawley Harvey Crippen in 1910, poisoner Frederick Seddon in 1912, and Herbert Rowse Armstrong, the only UK solicitor to ever be hanged for murder, in 1922. Now, on this frigid winter morning, he was at Holloway Prison to oversee the first execution of a woman in England since 1907.

Twenty-nine-year-old Edith Thompson had been sentenced to death the previous December for the murder of her husband, Percy. Her lover and alleged co-conspirator, Frederick Bywaters, was also scheduled to hang that morning at Pentonville Prison less than a mile away. Bywaters would go to his death stoically, but Mrs.

Thompson's execution was destined to give the witnesses nightmares for years to come.

As he approached the condemned cell, Ellis heard a deep moan. He found a petite, attractive brunette lying on the floor in a semi-conscious state. Two warders (as prison guards were called in the UK) bent over her, speaking gently, but her only response was a series of groans. Ellis recalled in his autobiography, "She looked dead already."

Working in tandem, the guards and Ellis' two assistants lifted Edith Thompson to her feet. After the hangman gently pinioned her wrists, she was carried the short distance from the condemned cell to the gallows. Because she was unable to stand, her escorts held her upright on the trap while Ellis applied straps to her ankles and thighs and fitted the noose around her neck. Then the lever was pulled, and Edith Thompson plunged to a mercifully quick death.

All that remained now was to confirm that her sentence had been carried out. Accompanied by the requisite medical professionals, Ellis went down the scaffold steps and parted the curtains that surrounded the now-hanging body. What he saw may have driven him to his eventual suicide.

Mrs. Thompson swayed silently, any reflexive tremors long since over. But on the floor beneath her feet was a widening pool of blood. It dripped down her legs, the flow too dark and heavy to be menstrual in origin.

Various explanations would be given for the sudden discharge: that she had been pregnant when executed and miscarried, or an earlier abortion had damaged her uterus so badly that the sudden drop of her body resulted in a hemorrhage. But no post-mortem was ever conducted to determine the cause, as the authorities wanted the matter to be forgotten as soon as possible.

The doctors stared in shock. John Ellis, who had completed nearly 200 executions by 1923, staggered out into the open, white-faced and gasping, "Oh Christ, oh Christ!"[8] His son would later say that Edith Thompson's execution haunted him until his own dying day.

******

Edith Jessie Thompson was known by several names during her short and tragic life. To her friends and family she was Edie, a cheerful and outgoing young woman

---

[8] From "Sentimentality to Abjection: The Case of Edith Thompson." Accessed May 28, 2015.

with such a knack for business that she became chief buyer for a British milliner. When her husband Percy was stabbed to death on a dark October night and a set of carelessly written letters appeared to connect her to the crime, she became the 'Messalina of Ilford'. Today, she is held up as the victim of a justice system that despised independent and successful women enough to let them hang for a crime they did not commit.

******

Edith Graydon was born on December 25, 1893 in Dalston, a working-class district in northeast London. Her father, William, was a clerk with the Imperial Tobacco Company and her mother, Ethel, was a policeman's daughter.

By all accounts her childhood was a happy one. She loved to dance and showed a rare acting ability, so perhaps she dreamed of a career on the stage like many imaginative girls do. But by the time she left school, any artistic aspirations were subdued in favor of a more practical career path.

Edith had been an excellent math student, so she easily found employment as a bookkeeper for Carlton &

White's, a London milliner and fabric importer. Her good looks and natural sense of style, combined with a high intelligence, resulted in an eventual promotion to chief buyer for the company. She made frequent trips to Paris to inspect new fabrics and make purchasing recommendations.

Not long after leaving school, sixteen-year-old Edith met Percy Thompson, who was three years her senior and worked in a shipping office. A year later they became engaged, but she was too young and career-ambitious to get married immediately. Their six-year engagement lasted until January 1915, when they were finally married. Soon afterward they purchased a home in the fashionable Essex town of Ilford and settled into a semi-affluent existence.

In 1921 a nineteen-year-old ship steward named Frederick Bywaters joined their social circle. Edith had known him for over nine years, as 'Freddy' and her younger brother had been school friends. Now she took special notice of him: Bywaters was handsome, outgoing, and worldly due to his extensive travel. Edith couldn't help comparing her husband unfavorably to him: Percy Thompson was staid and practical, with any sense of romance long gone.

"The circumstances of the marriage were in themselves not conducive to happiness," Filson Young wrote in *Notable British Trials*. "Husband and wife earned their living separately. They left the house at a quarter past eight in the morning and did not return until seven in the evening. There were no children, and they had thus practically nothing in common except the dormitory side of existence, which seems to have resolved itself into a chapter of bitter squabblings, and the deeper trouble that underlies the persistent attempts of a husband to take as a right something that should only be given."[9]

Bywaters joined the Thompsons and Edith's sister Avis on an extended visit to the Isle of Wight in June 1921. The foursome had such a good time together that when the group vacation ended, Percy Thompson invited the young steward to lodge with them whenever he was not at sea.

Edith couldn't have been more delighted. She and Bywaters began an affair soon afterward. When Thompson found out in August, he allegedly seized his wife, struck her several times, and threw her across the room before Bywaters could rush between them. The

---

[9] Bywaters, Frederick Edward Francis, and Edith Thompson. *Trial of Frederick Bywaters and Edith Thompson,* p.xv

confrontation between the two men ended with Bywaters being ordered out of the house on August 5.

He reluctantly left, but urged Edith to get a divorce or at least leave her husband. She demurred, saying she worried about the scandal, but in reality Edith Thompson didn't despise Percy enough to end the marriage. She was financially well off, and not in a hurry to jeopardize that. Sleeping with the young and handsome Bywaters satisfied her cravings for sex and romance, but she saw no real future in a life with her younger brother's former playmate.

When Bywaters left England for a month-long assignment on September 9, the lovers maintained a steady correspondence. She called him 'Darlint' and signed each letter with the nickname 'Peidi'. She was waiting for him when he returned in October, relishing the romantic escape he represented. Each time he went away (there would be two more trips before October 1922), Edith wrote frequently, and greeted him eagerly when he got back.

She gave Bywaters the impression that she was living a lie with her husband. In a letter dated March 31, 1922, she wrote:

After tonight I am going to die...not really...but put on the mask again darlint (sic) until the 26th May. Doesn't it seem years and years away? It does to me and I'll hope and hope all the time that I'll never have to wear the mask any more after this time . . . . This time really will be the last you will go away like things are, won't it? We said it before darlint I know and we failed . . . but there will be no failure this next time darlint, there mustn't be, I'm telling you. If things are the same again then I am going with you wherever it is....You'll never leave me behind again, never, unless things are different.

Left to right: Freddy Bywaters, Percy Thompson, Edith Thompson (Author's Collection)

Edith also led Bywaters to believe that she had tried to free herself by killing Percy. In a letter dated April 30, she claimed that she had smashed a glass light bulb, ground the pieces up, and mixed them in her husband's serving of mashed potatoes. On another occasion she 'admitted' to poisoning his food.

Many of these escapades she described were identical to scenes out of popular novels. Freddy Bywaters would later say that he never believed she had actually done any of these things. Edith Thompson had a flair for the melodramatic, and for her, writing about a murder attempt would diffuse the urge to act on it. Unfortunately, these letters were destined to be heard by a jury who did not know her well enough to make that distinction.

The infatuated youth confronted Percy Thompson and demanded that he give Edith a divorce. Thompson snapped, "I don't see how it concerns you."

"You are making Edie's life a hell. You know she is not happy with you."

"Well, I have got her and I am going to keep her."

Bywaters decided that the only way he and the woman he loved could be together was to get Thompson out of the picture. By any means necessary.

******

October 3, 1922 was a cool fall day. That evening, the Thompsons went to the Criterion Theatre in Piccadilly Circus to see a play with another couple, the Laxtons.

Percy and Edith did not get back to Ilford until midnight. As they walked along the deserted, lamp-lit Belgrade Road toward their Kensington Gardens home, they suddenly heard a set of footsteps hurrying toward them from behind.

It was Bywaters. To Thompson he snarled, "You have got to separate from your wife."

"No!"

The young steward lunged. He later said that Thompson moved as if about to go for a gun, so he took out a knife he always carried. During the struggle that followed, he stabbed his rival several times. After his arrest he told the police, "The reason I fought Thompson is because he never acted like a man to his wife. I could not go on seeing her live like she did. I did not intend to kill but only to injure him."

People living in the vicinity heard Edith scream and cry out, "No, don't!" When Thompson collapsed, Bywaters ran.

Dora Pittard, who was walking along Belgrave Road en route to her home in Endsleigh Gardens, was shocked to see Mrs. Thompson rush out of the dark toward her.

"Oh, my God, will you help me? My husband is ill—he is bleeding!"

Miss Pittard and a man who had been strolling nearby accompanied her back to where Thompson was slumped against a low stone wall, blood trickling from his mouth. They summoned a local physician named Maudsley, who arrived to find Thompson dead from multiple stab wounds and Edith in a state of advanced hysteria.

She told the doctor and the police that they had been walking home from Ilford train station when Thompson suddenly collapsed with a groan. When the police surgeon undressed the body at the morgue and saw the extent of the knife wounds, two sergeants from the Metropolitan Police's K Division went to the Thompson home to question the widow further.

Bywaters was also tracked down and interviewed, as his antagonism toward Percy Thompson was not secret. When Edith saw her young lover at the station, she assumed that he was confessing and sobbed, "Why did he do it? I didn't want him to do it. I must tell the truth. I saw my husband struggling with Freddy Bywaters."

Bywaters was arrested for murder. A search of his room revealed more than sixty letters from Edith Thompson. All it took was a brief perusal of their contents to transform the new widow from witness to suspect.

One read:

Yes, darlint you are jealous of him but I want you to be: he has the right by law to all that you have the right to by nature and love. Yes darlint, be jealous, so much that you will do something desperate.

These letters were the only real evidence linking Edith Thompson to her husband's death, but it was enough to get her arrested. British law dictated that if two people want to kill a third, and one of the conspirators acts on the expressed intentions of both, both are equally guilty of murder.

At first Bywaters denied all knowledge of the attack, but when informed that Mrs. Thompson was being charged too, he was astonished.

"Why Mrs. Thompson? She was not aware of my movements."

The couple was put on trial two months later, on December 6, at the Old Bailey, which was London's criminal courthouse. When Bywaters took the stand, the prosecution showed him passages from the letters that referred to a plot or shared purpose. Asked if the plot concerned the murder of Edith's husband, he shook his head and said that Edith had been talking about a suicide pact, something that figured prominently in the romance novels she devoured. The premise was that if Thompson would not give her a divorce, she and her lover would die together rather than live separately.

"She had a vivid way of declaring herself," he said at one point. "She would read a book and imagine herself as the character in the book."

Bywaters reiterated that Edith Thompson had been unaware of his plans that night and that his initial aim was to confront her husband. When Thompson reacted in a condescending manner, Bywaters saw red.

Edith's father, William Graydon, also insisted that some of the letters were nothing more than products of his daughter's imagination. One missive dated June 23, 1922 stated that Thompson had exposed Freddy and

Edith's affair to her father. When portions of it were read in the courtroom, Graydon was astonished.

"Thompson never came to me and made any complaint as to the conduct of my daughter with Bywaters," he said. "That is the purest imagination."

Edith's sister, Avis Graydon, was asked about certain events that she supposedly played a part in. She shook her head in disbelief. "That is all my sister's imagination."

When it was Edith's turn to testify, she proved to be a terrible witness. Her self-pitying and melodramatic responses made a bad impression on the judge and jury, and admitting to lying about the circumstances of her husband's murder didn't help either.

"I was very agitated, and I did not want to say anything against Mr. Bywaters," she protested. "I wanted to shield him."

Filson Young, who attended the trial, did not believe that she had ever tried to kill Percy Thompson. He wrote, "It is certainly inconsistent with her character, as I conceive it, that if she had really intended to poison her husband she would have philandered with the idea on paper, and written reams of incriminating matter. She would have done it, and said (or written) nothing about it. A Borgia does not write; she acts."

The judge, Mr. Justice Shearman, summed up the case for the jury in a manner that was fair where points of law were concerned. Referring to Edith Thompson, he said, "You will not convict her unless you are satisfied that she and he agreed that this man should be murdered when he could be, and she knew that he was going to do it, and directed him to do it, and by arrangement between them he was doing it."

But his distaste for the adulterous antics of both defendants was obvious. Shearman described Mrs. Thompson's letters as "full of the outpourings of a silly but at the same time, a wicked affection."

On December 11, after a two-hour deliberation, the jury returned a verdict of guilty. When Justice Shearman pronounced the death sentence on both defendants, Edith dissolved into hysterics while Bywaters loudly protested her innocence.

******

During the trial, the press and public were highly critical of both Bywaters and Thompson, but once the pair had been sentenced to death, universal attitudes abruptly shifted. Many claimed that hanging a woman was an abhorrent act, and others admired Freddy Bywaters for his devotion to the woman he loved. Nearly a million people signed a petition urging William Bridgeman, the Home Secretary, to commute the death sentences to life in prison.

Edith's family was allowed to see her at the Old Bailey holding cell the night she was convicted. She was still unhinged, screaming and crying. When she saw her father she broke away from her police escorts, seized him, and wailed, "Dad, take me home!"

It was widely expected that she would not be executed. Even John Ellis, the hangman, was convinced that there would be a reprieve. "I never dreamt Mrs. Thompson would hang," he said. "I really believed the authorities would bow before the storm of protest from the public."

An autopsy on Percy Thompson had failed to turn up evidence that he had ever been poisoned or consumed ground glass. This created universal concern that the assassination attempts outlined in Mrs. Thompson's letters really were the work of a bored and imaginative wife.

Edith spent most of the time between the conviction and execution in the Holloway Prison hospital, alternating between apathy and full-blown hysterics. She rallied when her parents and legal advisors told her about the reprieve campaign. Although the prospect of spending years—if not the rest of her life—in prison still frightened her, the thought that her life might be saved calmed her enough to start eating again.

It was not to be, however. Despite the petition and Bywaters' insistence that Edith Thompson had nothing to do with his actions, the Home Secretary did not commute her sentence. When informed of the decision and the fixed execution date, her composure evaporated and she spent her remaining days screaming, moaning, and crying.

Those attending her were also affected, believing that a miscarriage of justice was about to take place. The prison chaplain, Reverend Glanville Murray, remembered, "When we were all gathered together there it seemed utterly impossible to believe what we were there to do...My God, the impulse to rush in and save her by force was almost too strong for me."[10]

---

[10] "From Sentimentality to Abjection: The Case of Edith Thompson." From Sentimentality to Abjection: The Case of Edith Thompson. Accessed

On the morning of her execution Edith was heavily sedated, but still agitated enough to moan and faint when John Ellis came for her. She couldn't walk without assistance, and was completely unconscious when the noose was fitted around her neck. A rumor circulated that she had to be hanged while positioned in a chair, whichwas not the case, but she had to be held upright until the moment the lever was pulled.

When her body plunged, there was a massive outpouring of blood from her uterus. There are strong indicators that she was pregnant: although she ate next to nothing during the three months in custody, her weight had gone up from 119 to 131 pounds. British law dictated that pregnant women under sentence of death received a stay of execution until they had given birth, so it's surprising that Edith did not 'plead her belly', as the saying went. Perhaps she assumed that the missed periods were due to stress.

Another theory was that she had undergone an abortion at some point, and been left with a badly damaged uterus. This condition, combined with the force of the drop through the trapdoor, may have caused her uterus to invert.

Whatever the cause of the vaginal hemorrhage, all women subsequently hanged in the UK were required to wear a canvas undergarment which would catch any similar blood flow and spare the official witnesses that same horrible spectacle.

Everyone present that cold January morning was affected by Edith's hanging. John Ellis was so distressed that he attempted suicide later. Dr. Morton, Governor of Holloway Prison, went to the offices of the *Daily Mail* that very night and urged the editor to start a campaign against the death penalty. The Deputy Governor, a Miss Cronin, was also reported as being deeply troubled by the entire affair. Some of the female guards quit their jobs.

Edith and Bywaters, who had gone to his death stoically, were buried on the grounds on their respective prisons. In 1971 her remains, along with those of three other female prisoners who had been hanged at Holloway before the death penalty was abolished in Britain, were exhumed and reburied in a single unmarked plot at Brookwood Cemetery in Brookwood, Surrey. It wasn't until the 1990s that a large granite tombstone marked Edith's final resting place.

*****

The execution of Edith Thompson disturbed the British public. Many argued that her letters had been proven to be figments of an overripe imagination and that she had really been hanged for being a childless adulteress and earning double the average national wage when former soldiers were struggling to find jobs. The popular press had called her the "Messalina of Ilford", and the Crown prosecutor had gone above and beyond his official duty to present her as a depraved threat to society who deserved to hang. Even the jury foreman, after reading her letters to his co-jurors, said later, "'Nauseous' is hardly strong enough to describe their contents...Mrs. Thompson's letters were her own condemnation."[11]

She and Bywaters joined the line-up of waxworks at Madame Tussauds and became a fast favorite with the museum's patrons. Even Alfred Hitchcock admitted to being fascinated with the Thompson-Bywaters affair, saying that he would welcome the opportunity to make a documentary film about the case. (He never did.)

---

[11] Nadine Attewell, *Better Britons: Reproduction, National Identity, and the Afterlife of Empire*, p. 124

In 1988 author and English professor Rene Weis published *Criminal Justice: The True Story of Edith Thompson*. The book was reissued in 2001 when a movie about the case, titled *Another Life*, was released. (Edith was played by veteran stage and film actress Natasha Little, while Nick Moran played Percy Thompson and Ioan Gruffudd of *Horatio Hornblower* fame played Freddy Bywaters.) Weis and others have been working intently to secure a posthumous pardon for Edith Thompson. His careful research for *Criminal Justice* was used as the basis of a submission to the Criminal Cases Review Commission, which investigates suspected miscarriages of justice. No pardon has been issued yet, but the campaign continues.

The makers of *Another Life* assert that Edith Thompson was executed for who she was, not what she did. And who had she been? A successful businesswoman who bobbed her hair, wore short skirts, and wrote freely about sex. British society in 1923 couldn't handle the way she thumbed her nose at its moral code, which contained strong traces of the not-so-distant Victorian era.

"Edith Thompson was a woman born in the wrong era and punished for it with her life," said Philip Goodhew, the director.

Unfortunately, death is irreversible.

"LET HIM HAVE IT"- THE TRAGEDY OF DEREK BENTLEY

"Let him have it!"

It's a phrase that's been immortalized in gangster movies and crime dramas. Gunfire always follows, and someone dies.

On the night of November 2, 1952, those words allegedly resulted in the death of a London police officer. Over three months later, a nineteen-year-old youth was hanged for uttering them.

Derek Bentley hadn't pulled the trigger, but the prosecutor claimed that he incited the person who did by yelling, "Let him have it, Chris!" Now, there is evidence that he hadn't even done that.

******

Derek Bentley. (Author's Collection)

Derek Bentley was born on June 30, 1933. His childhood years were plagued by mental health issues; when a bomb struck his house during World War II, the brick structure collapsed around him, resulting in serious head injuries. He did poorly in school and experienced his first arrest in March 1948, when he and another boy were charged with theft. In September 1948 he was sentenced to three years at the Kingswood Approved School outside Bristol.

School authorities administered diagnostic tests that estimated the fifteen year old boy's mental age to be 10 years old. Another test showed his IQ to be a mere 66. Other test results were just as dismal: an EEG reading indicated that he was epileptic and his reading ability was in line with that of a five-year-old.

Upon his release in July 1950, Bentley became a recluse, staying home and cutting ties to the few friends he had. In 1952, when he was nineteen and eligible for mandatory national service, the doctors pronounced him 'mentally substandard' and therefore unfit for military life.

Urged by his family to get a job, Bentley found employment at a furniture removal company but was forced to leave after hurting his back a year later. When he healed enough to move without experiencing pain, he joined the Croydon Corporation as a garbage collector, but his limited mobility and spotty attention span got him demoted to street cleaner within three months. In September 1952 they finally fired him.

Frustrated and depressed, nineteen-year-old Bentley tried to get money the only way that had worked for him in the past. On the night of November 2, 1952, he met up with Christopher Craig, a sixteen-year-old fellow delinquent. Their original plan was to rob a butcher shop, but the closed establishment remained so well-lit that they withdrew. Undeterred, they chose a second target: the warehouse of Barlow & Parker, a confectionary manufacturer and wholesaler in Croydon.

Both youths were armed. Craig had a Colt New Service .455 Eley calibre revolver, whose barrel he had sawed off so that it would be easier to conceal. Bentley was carrying a spiked knuckleduster and a knife, both of which his younger friend had given him.

Unfortunately for the would-be robbers, a nine-year-old girl living across the road happened to be looking out her bedroom window and saw them jump over the warehouse gate. When they clambered up a drainpipe to the roof, she alerted her father, who hurried to the closest telephone box and called the police.

When a police team arrived, Craig hissed, "It's a copper! Hide behind here!"

He and Bentley ducked behind a shelter on the roof and waited. Around ten minutes later Detective Sergeant Frederick Fairfax appeared and shouted, "I am a police officer! This place is surrounded!"

Spying the two young men, Fairfax ran over and seized Bentley. Turning toward Craig, who had pulled out his revolver, he then said, "Hand over the gun, lad."

Bentley struggled free and allegedly yelled to his friend, "Let him have it, Chris!!'

Craig opened fire, the bullet grazing Fairfax's shoulder. Other policemen appeared and opened fire, turning the rooftop into a battle zone.

Police Constable Sidney Miles hurried up the stairs leading to the roof. The 22-year veteran of the Metropolitan Police Force had gotten building keys from the manager and was on his way to Fairfax's assistance. When he stepped through the rooftop door, a bullet struck him in the head, killing him instantly.

Although he could have pulled out his knuckleduster or knife and easily overpowered the injured Fairfax, Bentley remained in place. Craig, on the other hand, ran after exhausting his ammunition. When more policemen surrounded him, he jumped off the roof. The thirty-foot fall broke his spine and left wrist, but he survived.

Both young men were charged with the murder of PC Miles. Derek Bentley's statement to the police read as follows:

I have been cautioned that I need not say anything unless I wish to do so, but whatever I do say will be taken down in writing and may be given in evidence.

(signed) Derek Bentley

I have known Craig since I went to school. We were stopped by our parents going out together, but we still continued going out with each other - I mean we have not gone out together until tonight. I was watching television tonight (2nd November 1952) and between 8pm and 9pm Craig called for me. My Mother answered the door and I heard her say I was out. I had been out earlier to the pictures and got home just after 7pm. A little later Norman Parsley and Frank Fazey called. I did not answer the door or speak to them.

My Mother told me that they had called and I then ran out after them. I walked up the road with them to the paper shop where I saw Craig standing. We all talked together and then Norman Parsley and Frank Fazey left. Chris Craig and I then caught a bus to Croydon. We got off at West Croydon and then walked down the road where the toilets are - I think it is Tamworth Road. When we came to the place where you found me, Chris looked in the window. There was a little iron gate at the side. Chris then jumped over and I followed. Up to then Chris had not said anything. We both got out on to the flat roof at the top. Then someone in a garden on the opposite side shone a torch up towards us. Chris said: "It's a copper, hide behind here." We hid behind a shelter arrangement on the roof. We were there waiting for about ten minutes. I did not know he was going to use the gun. A plain clothes man climbed up the drainpipe and on to the roof. The man said: "I am a police officer - the place is surrounded." He caught hold of me (and) as we walked away Chris fired. There was nobody else there at the time. The policeman and I went round a corner by a door. A little later the door opened and a policeman in uniform came out. Chris fired again then and this policeman fell down. I could see he was hurt as a lot of blood came from his forehead just above his nose.

The policeman dragged him round the corner behind the brickwork entrance to the door. I remember I shouted something but I forget what it was. I could not see Chris when I shouted to him - he was behind a wall. I heard some more policemen behind the door and the policeman with me said, "I don't think he has many more bullets left." Chris shouted "Oh yes I have" and he fired again. I think I heard him fire three times altogether. The Policeman then pushed me down the stairs and I did not see any more. I knew we were going to break into the place, I did not know what we were going to get - just anything that was going. I did not have a gun and I did not know Chris had one until he shot. I now know that the policeman in uniform is dead. I should have mentioned that after the plain clothes policeman got up the drainpipe and arrested me, another policeman in uniform followed and I heard someone call him 'Mac'. He was with us when the other policeman was killed.

This statement has been read to me and is true.

(signed) Derk [sic] Derek W. Bentley

Statement taken by me, written down by Det Sgt Shepherd, read over and signature witness by J. Smith DI.

The murder trial began at the Old Bailey on December 9, 1952. Public feeling ran high against the defendants, since the general belief in 1952 was that youth gangs were terrorizing London, and murdering anyone who tried to stop them. The year before, four police officers had been killed in the line of duty, and people muttered that *someone* had to pay for the death of PC Miles.

Both Craig and Bentley pleaded not guilty before Lord Goddard, the Lord Chief Justice. Although Derek Bentley had not fired the fatal bullet or even resisted arrest, the case against him hinged on one main issue.

British law stated that if two or more people are involved in a crime, they can all be held equally liable when there is evidence of a common purpose. The now infamous phrase "Let him have it, Chris!" were introduced as proof that both young men intended to kill a police officer.

The defence argued that Bentley had never made such a statement. (The police were the only ones to ever claim that he did.) The nineteen-year-old defendant's solicitor pointed out that even if he had, he could just as likely have meant, "Give him the gun."

Ambiguity existed over the number of shots fired as well as by whom. The bullet that had killed PC Miles was never found, and a ballistics expert later stated that the sawed-off barrel on Craig's gun would have affected his ability to hit an object at a certain range. The teenager's solicitor stressed to the jury that the veteran policeman could just as easily have been killed by friendly fire.

Derek Bentley's capacity to stand trial had been questioned at first. A psychiatrist at Maudsley Hospital stated that the youth was illiterate and borderline retarded, but the Principal Medical Officer (head of the country's medical services) testified that while Bentley's intelligence was low, he was not a 'feeble-minded' person under the Mental Deficiency Act. Although Scottish law recognized the concept of diminished capacity due to mental impairment, English law did not, and would not until the passage of the Homicide Act 1957. The only accepted medical defence to a murder charge was criminal insanity, and Bentley was not insane.

Lord Goddard made much of the fact that Bentley had been armed with a knife and knuckleduster (even though Craig had supplied him with both weapons) and gone voluntarily to the warehouse to commit a potentially violent crime. His summing-up made it clear that he had no doubt of their guilt.

At one point Goddard said, "...see what Bentley had on him. Where is that knuckleduster?" When it was handed to him he actually put it on before continuing:

Apparently it was given to him by Craig, but Bentley was armed with this knuckleduster. Have you ever seen a more horrible sort of weapon? You know, this is to hit a person in the face with who comes at you. You grasp it here, your fingers go through—I cannot quite get mine through, I think—and you have got a dreadful heavy steel bar to strike anybody with; and you can kill a person with this, of course. Then did you ever see a more shocking thing than that? You have got a spike with which you can jab anybody who comes at you; if the blow with the steel is not enough, you have got this spike at the side to jab. You can have it to see, if you like, when you go to your room. It is a shocking weapon. Here was Craig armed with a revolver and that sheath knife. Hand me that sheath knife—the big one. One wonders, really, what parents can be about in these days, allowing a boy of 16—they say, perhaps, they do not know, but why don't they know?—to have a weapon like this which he takes about with him? It is not a new one, you can see; it is pretty well worn. That was the thing that Craig was talking about. Where is the other knife? Here is Bentley with a smaller knife, but you can feel it is sharp and pointed. What is he carrying that with him for in his coat, not even with a sheath on it?[12]

It took the jury only 75 minutes to find Christopher Craig and Derek Bentley guilty of murder. Because he was under eighteen, Craig was sentenced to be detained in prison "at Her Majesty's Pleasure" while nineteen-year-old Bentley received the death penalty.

Although the jury recommended mercy in Bentley's case, Lord Goddard did not do the same in his post-trial report to the Home Office. In August 1970 he told author David Yallop that he thought Bentley would be reprieved and his own input was unnecessary.

The oversight proved fatal to the condemned youth. The Court of Appeal dismissed Bentley's petition on January 13, 1953, concluding that if the trial justice saw no reason to recommend a reprieve, they had no grounds to interfere either.

Derek Bentley's fate was now in the hands of the Home Secretary, Sir David Maxwell Fife.

---

[12] David Yallop, *To Encourage the Others*, p. 398

******

William Bentley, Derek's father, created a public awareness campaign that did much to create sympathy for his son. Supporters argued that Bentley's impaired mental state and low IQ made him an easy dupe for the intelligent and domineering Craig. He had only been carrying deadly weapons because his younger friend had given them to him in the first place.

Fife ultimately refused to grant the reprieve. Bentley's family and friends figured that the Home Secretary wanted someone to pay for the police constable's murder and pose a deterrent to future offenders. Since Craig could not be subject to the death penalty, Derek Bentley drew the short straw.

The public was appalled at the injustice and even Parliament got involved, with over 200 MPs signing a petition urging the Home Secretary to reconsider. It stated:

We the undersigned members of the Commons House of Parliament, believing the advice tendered by you to her Majesty the Queen in the case of Derek Bentley to be grievously mistaken and out of accord with the natural justice of the case, respectfully urge that even now you will advise her Majesty to exercise the royal prerogative of mercy so that the sentence of death on him be not executed.

William Bentley, accompanied by Christopher Craig's mother, went to the Home Office to beg the Secretary of State to reconsider, but a representative informed the stricken father that the decision was final.

Crowds assembled outside the House of Commons and Whitehall, yelling, "Bentley must not die" and "Bentley must be reprieved". When police officers barred the Home Office entrance, the protestors were undeterred; they moved on to Sir David Maxwell-Fyfe's home and to Downing Street. They kept it up until just after 2:00 a.m., fighting with the police whenever their demonstrations were thwarted.

On the morning of the hanging, January 28, a huge crowd gathered outside Wandsworth Prison. By all accounts, Derek Bentley went quietly to his death and the hangman, Albert Pierpont, did a clean job. But if the Lord Goddard, the Home Secretary, and anyone else who supported the execution hoped the young man would be forgotten, they were completely wrong...

******

Derek Bentley's sister, Iris, had just turned twenty-one when her brother was hanged. She was so determined to clear his name that she broke off her engagement to help her parents in the crusade. Iris Bentley kept up the battle for decades, even when faced with a cancer diagnosis. She later said that the drive to get a posthumous pardon for Derek kept her going through painful treatments and operations.

In October 1992 Home Secretary Kenneth Clarke responded to her request. The file she had prepared contained new evidence collected from witnesses who had never testified at the trial, and even included a statement from Christopher Craig himself. Craig, now fifty-five and a plumbing engineer with a family, swore that Derek Bentley had never said, "Let him have it!"

Incredibly, Clarke denied the petition. He said that Bentley's mental incapacity and the fact that he had not actually shot PC Miles should have resulted in a reprieve, not a declaration of innocence. In his view, a royal pardon was out of the question.

Christopher Craig was so distraught that he drew the curtains at his Bedfordshire home and went into seclusion. Politicians and campaigners expressed their disgust. Iris, after composing herself, vowed to fight on.

"I'll never, never give up," she declared. "I can see Derek saying 'Come on sis, there's an awful lot to do'....When I die I want that piece of paper, that pardon, put with me in my coffin. I am a very strong believer in an afterlife and I want to be able to show it to Derek and my parents when we meet again."[13]

A partial victory was obtained the following year, when the new Home Secretary, Michael Howard, granted a 'limited posthumous pardon'. It stated that Bentley should not have been executed, but did not absolve him of guilt. It was close to what Derek's supporters were after, but not enough.

Iris died of cancer in January 1997, but her daughter Maria kept the campaign alive. In April 1997 she presented the case to the Criminal Cases Review Commission, who decided there was enough evidence to refer it to the Court of Appeal.

---

[13] Mills, Heather. "Hanged Man's Sister Sees Hopes Shattered." *The Independent*. October 2, 1992.

The Court heard the case from July 20 to 24, 1998. On the 30th, they issued a judgement declaring that Derek Bentley's conviction had been "unsafe".

Lord Thomas Bingham, the Chief Justice, was severe in his criticism of Lord Goddard's summing-up. It was, he said, "such as to deny the appellant that fair trial which is the birthright of every British citizen....It must be a matter of profound and continuing regret that this mistrial occurred and that the defects we have found were not recognised at the time."

Derek Bentley's conviction was therefore set aside. One reporter pointed out that if he had still been alive in 1998, he would have been eligible for a retrial.

Christopher Craig could barely contain his emotion.

"While I am grateful and relieved about this (the quashed conviction), I am saddened that it has taken those 46 years for the authorities in this country to admit the truth," he told the press. "I am truly sorry that my actions on 2 November 1952 caused so much pain and misery for the family of PC Miles, who died that night doing his duty....A day does not go by when I don't think about Derek and now his innocence has been proved with this judgment. Now at last this case is over. My gratitude goes to those who have fought so tirelessly for justice."[14]

******

Bentley's story inspired books, songs like Elvis Costello's 'Let Him Dangle' and 'Let Him Have It' by the Bureau, and a 1991 movie, *Let Him Have It*, starring Christopher Eccleston (of *Dr. Who* fame) as Bentley and Paul Reynolds as Craig.

More significantly, the young man's execution was pivotal in ending capital punishment in the UK. It took nearly half a century, but finally the UK justice system formally acknowledged what had always been common knowledge: that Derek Bentley died an innocent man.

---

[14] "Craig's Relief at Bentley Pardon." BBC News. July 30, 1998. Accessed June 7, 2015.

CONCLUSION

Some mistakes are like time itself: no matter how much you might wish otherwise, they cannot be reversed.

Modern headlines are full of stories about people being released from death row after years spent waiting for execution. This reminds us that people like Eliza Fenning, Edith Thompson, and Derek Bentley were put to death because exculpatory evidence was either not available or was studiously ignored at their trials.

Eliza Fenning was a servant at a time when people in England still remembered the French Revolution and how the lower classes had massacred their social betters, creating a fear of subversive domestics. Edith Thompson was a childless woman with a flourishing career and a lover eight years her junior, which offended still-extant Victorian morality. Derek Bentley stood trial for murdering a policeman after a wave of youth crime left Londoners frightened and vengeful.

From the moment they entered their respective courtrooms, these vulnerable people never really stood a chance. By extension, we must consider the thousands worldwide who are presently imprisoned, awaiting a similar fate. Many people feel the death penalty should be abolished, and even those who support it agree that it must not be used unless the evidence is irrefutable. If the death penalty is to be applied, it should be based on what the defendant did, not what they represent to society at large

EXCERPTS FROM JACK SMITH'S BOOK SERIAL KILLERS EXPLORING THE HORRIFIC CRIMES OF LITTLE KNOWN MURDERERS

Introduction

One of the strangest, most terrifying, and most fascinating aspects of our society is the existence of serial killers. There is an important distinction to be made between mass murderers and serial killers. The mass murderer commits multiple murders on one occasion, whereas the serial killer will murder on more than a single occasion and at different places. While murderers have existed for many centuries, the term serial killer is a contemporary construction. Many attribute the first use of the term to FBI agent Robert Ressler during a lecture he gave in 1974 in England. From an historic point of view, the first recording of serial killers can traced back all the way to Jack the Ripper, who terrorized women of the night in nineteenth century London. At the time, these brutal murders became front-page fodder for the newly popular newspaper industry. With people craving information about even the most horrifying of deaths, the idea of a killer addicted to murder was born. Since then, thousands of individuals have taken on the mantle of "Serial Killer," feeding into society's fascination with these strange and brutal people.

From John Wayne Gacy to Jeffrey Dahmer, many of America's most famous murderers have entered into the collective cultural consciousness. They have become pop culture figures, famous for their crimes and the violent nature of their acts. People feel compelled to understand more about these dark and twisted crimes, even when they disgust. For audiences everywhere, the very idea that these people can exist and operate in day-to-day life becomes an issue of abject terror and interest. That your neighbor, your boss, or your gas station attendant might be in the midst of a killing spree taps into something primal and very hard to imagine. It reflects the darkest side of the human psyche.

"Serial Killer" as a term can be difficult to define. Different criminal investigation units typically require two, three, or more attributable killings over a period of time before an individual can be considered to have joined the ranks of the serial killers. However, it is not really the numbers which can interest so many people and scare others. Instead, it is the often random nature of the killings. Rather than crimes of passion, crimes of financial reward, or instances when an individual has reached their end of their emotional tether, the crimes of serial killers have often been planned days, weeks, or months in advance. Targets can be random, but the killings are often planned in great detail. From cannibalism to mental health concerns, from ritualistic witchcraft to a simple interest in violence, learning what motivates these people can offer both insight and further confusion.

It speaks volumes that for every serial killer operating at any point in the world the amount of film, television, and literature focused on fictional versions is huge. From Hannibal Lecter to Patrick Bateman, these figures are often disguised metaphors for our own culture or the ways in which we interpret and react to the horrors of their real life equivalents. Serial killers, both real and fictional, are big business. They are reported on the news, make the front page of papers, and in films, which often, when based on their lives, top the box office. If there is one quality that is shared by all serial killers, it is the fact that we as a society are fascinated and appalled in equal measure.

With that in mind, anyone who has spent time looking into the subject probably knows everything there is to know about the typical rogues' gallery of mass murderers. Ted Bundy, Gary Ridgway, and Harold Shipman have all been front page news in America, the United Kingdom, and beyond. Their actions have become infamous because of their nature. But they are not alone. One former member of the FBI, John Douglas, suggested that there could be as many as thirty-five serial killers active at any one time in the United States alone. Expand these figures globally and some of the most monstrous murderers of all can sneak under the radar. In this book, we will take a look at some of the lesser-known serial killers, looking beyond the pale of conventional knowledge and discovering more about what drives these individuals towards such heinous acts. Read on and learn more about some of the most violent, chilling, and captivating individuals to have ever existed, history's hidden serial killers.

The isolated loner who butchered women and scattered their remains across Alaska

Robert Hansen

Also known as the Butcher Baker"

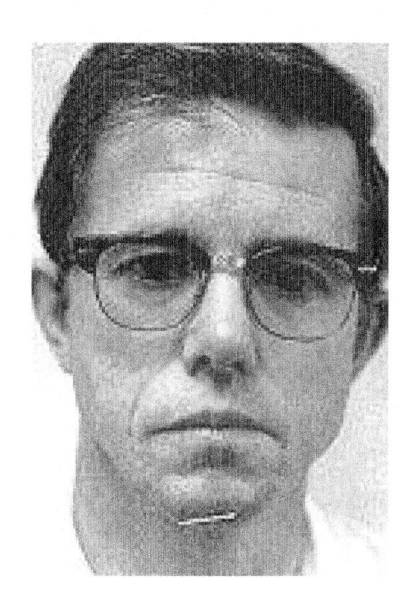

The setting

For many people, understanding the mind of the serial killer depends on being able to understand their childhood. For those who might think an upbringing of rejection and resentment helps create these individuals, the case of the Butcher Baker might be the archetypal example.

Robert Hansen was born in 1939 in Esterville, Iowa. His parents had recently emigrated from Denmark, and the young Robert was destined to step into his father's profession as a baker. Those who knew him as a child described Robert as "painfully shy;" his skinny frame, stutter, and severe bout of ace left him scarred physically and emotionally. His appearance meant he was shunned by the more attractive members of the opposite sex, forging a resentment which boiled and bubbled beneath the surface of Hansen's character. Increasingly dysfunctional and isolated, his relationships with family members – his father in particular – became strained. A victim of bullying and without the familial support others might have enjoyed, Robert Hansen took to hunting. It gave him a relief from his circumstances. He became quite the talented marksman. With this in mind, he enlisted himself in the Army Reserves, serving for one year before being discharged from the military. Similar positions as a police academy assistant drill instructor followed, during which time he met a young girl and fell in love. The pair married in 1960.

The first inklings of a darker side of Robert came to the fore in December of that year. After an arson attempt on a garage containing the local school bus, Robert was arrested and sentenced to twenty months of a three year stint in prison. His wife, not thinking this to be the man she married, sought to divorce her new husband. Robert served his time but, upon release, found himself alone again. He began to steal, serving minor prison sentences for petty theft. In 1967, having met another woman he intended to marry, they decided to move to Alaska. Now with two children in tow, the move to Anchorage seemed a shot at redemption for Robert, with his new neighbors admitting to warming to the man. He even managed to impress the locals with his hunting prowess, winning several awards for his marksmanship. He followed in his father's footsteps and became a baker. Everything seemed to be going well for Robert and his family, but it was not meant to last. During 1977, Robert was arrested and thrown in jail following the theft of a chainsaw. During this time, he was diagnosed by mental health professionals as having bipolar disorder. To combat this, he was given a prescription for lithium but was never under any official instructions to take the drug.

His crimes

Perhaps the most famous incident involving Robert Hansen (and the one about which we have the most detail) involves an attempted murder on June 13, 1983. A young girl named Cindy Paulson managed to escape from a man who has been trying to shove her into the rear of his vehicle. Cindy, a seventeen-year-old, had been offered two hundred dollars to engage in a sex act with the man who had then drawn a gun on her and forced her to a home in the nearby area of Muldoon. Here, the man turned her into his captive. Cindy was repeatedly tortured, raped, assaulted, and kept chained to the wall by her neck while her captor slept. The man was Robert Hansen.

When her captor woke from his slumber, he stowed Cindy in his vehicle and drove to the nearby Merrill Field Aiport. Here, Robert informed his victim that they were to visit his 'cabin' – in actuality, this cabin was a meat shack near the Knik River which was only reachable using a boat or a small plane. This is when Cindy planned her escape. Bundled into the back seat of the car, her hands tied together, she was forced to wait until her attacker was no longer paying attention. As soon as her moment arrived, she crept out of the back seat and began to run, fleeing Hansen when his back was turned. At this point, she was not wearing her shoes. Crucially, she had decided to leave her sneakers behind in the back seat of the car. This would act as an indication to the police that she had indeed been held captive in the vehicle. Noticing his escaped captive, Hansen began to chase the girl. Before he could catch her, however, she had flagged down a passing truck and convinced the driver to pull over. With her disheveled and understandably terrified demeanor, the driver felt compelled to drive her to a local inn, wherein she pleaded with the front desk clerk to use their phone. She called her boyfriend while her savior – the truck driver – drove on to work. He would later inform the police of the incident.

Once the police arrived at Cindy's location, they were informed that she had telephoned a taxi and had driven to her boyfriend's place of work, a nearby motel. Officers found her there, handcuffed, afraid, and alone. She was taken to the local police headquarters and asked to make a statement. Details of her captor were given. Police who questioned Robert Hansen found that he denied any involvement, with the man suggesting to police that the girl was lying and possibly trying to extort him. Thinking Hansen not much more than a meek-mannered baker, and noting his confirmed alibi given by a friend, the police did not consider Robert Hansen to be a suspect in the kidnapping, rape, and torture of Cindy Paulson. Hansen was allowed to walk free.

At this time, Alaskan State Troopers had set up an investigation into the origin of a number of bodies discovered throughout the Anchorage area. These bodies had been found by locals and investigated by police, with many of the corpses never wholly identified. The lead investigator, Glenn Flothe, noticed the connection between the three killings and the similar manner of death in all three cases. Thinking there might be a killer on the loose, he requested additional assistance. Authorities constructed a psychological profile based on the recovered bodies, noting that the handiwork seemed that of an experienced and skilled hunter, one who might suffer from low self-esteem and who had been rejected in the past by the opposite sex. Particularly of interest was the killer's penchant for keeping "souvenirs" from each of his victims. These trophies included jewelry and other identifying marks. Perhaps most accurately of all, the profile even indicated that the killer might possess a stammer or stutter. Armed with this profile and the recent investigations into the capture of Cindy Paulson, Flothe began to work his way through the list. Eventually he worked his way to Robert Hensen, the experienced hunter with a stutter who owned a small plane.

The State Troopers obtained a warrant and searched Hansen's vehicles and home. As well as an arsenal of guns, they found several small items of jewelry, confirmed as belonging to the victims. One of the most important discoveries was a map hidden behind the suspect's headboard. Hansen has marked several small "x" notations all across the local countryside. Even though he was presented with a wealth of evidence, Hansen continued to deny any involvement. He blamed the women for trying to extort him and even tried to justify his actions. Finally, he confessed completely to a list of murders and the evidence presented to him. His list of victims even went back beyond the prostitutes and strippers who had led investigators to his capture, including sixteen- to nineteen-year-old girls who had not been found. Thanks to the one escaped victim and the work of the police, Robert Hansen was apprehended in 1983.

The Sentence

The first charges brought against Hansen were assault, numerous weapons citations, kidnapping, and even insurance fraud. This last charge related to the supposed theft of a number of his sporting trophies, the claimed insurance money having been put towards purchasing his vehicle. When speaking at his own trial,

Hansen recalled discovering the trophies at a later date but confessed that he did not inform the insurance company. The evidence against him began to mount up. Ballistics reports tied Hansen's weapons to the bullets found at numbers crime scenes. Eventually, Hansen entered a plea bargain. He admitted to his role in four killings of young women – those cases for which the police had evidence – and provided evidence leading to the discovery of the remains of his other victims. In exchange, Hansen would serve his time in a federal prison, and press attention would be restricted. Finally, he agreed to help decipher the small marks on the map found behind his headboard, helping grieving families locate their daughters' remains. Seventeen gravesites were located in all, a least a dozen of which had been unknown to the authorities. They covered a huge amount of South Central Alaska. Despite cooperation, there remained three notations on the map that Hansen would not reveal. The police suspect that these belonged to Mary Thill and Megan Emrick, killings in which Hansen denied any involvement.

Discussing his style of killing with the police, Hansen confessed to occasionally letting his victims go if they managed to convince him that they would not report him to the authorities. Tracing back his history of violence, he confessed that he had begun his murder spree as early as the start of the 1970s. The final sentence passed down from the judge was four hundred and sixty one years without the possibility of parole. While many of his victims' bodies have been recovered, the full extent of Robert Hansen's sadism has not been revealed. Despite over a decade of killing, his actions have largely escaped the collective cultural consciousness. This could be due to the remote Alaskan location or the plea bargain the serial killer struck. Perhaps it is encouraging to note the accuracy of the psychological profile constructed of the Baker Butcher, as Hansen was later known, and its importance in his capture.

OTHER BOOKS FROM JACK SMITH

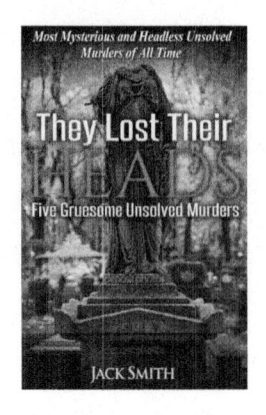

SOURCES

Eliza Fenning

Dickens, Charles, and Georgina Hogarth. *The Letters of Charles Dickens*. London: Macmillan and, 1893.

Fenning, Elizabeth, and Robert Turner. *Affecting Case of Eliza Fenning, Who Suffered the Sentence of the Law, July 26, 1815*. London: John Fairburn, 1815.

May, Allyson N. *The Bar and the Old Bailey, 1750-1850*. Chapel Hill: University of North Carolina Press, 2003.

The Massalina of Ilford

Attewell, Nadine. *Better Britons: Reproduction, National Identity, and the Afterlife of Empire*. Toronto, Ontario: University of Toronto Press, 2014.

Weis, Rene. *Criminal Justice: The True Story of Edith Thompson*. London: Hamish Hamilton, 1988.

Young, Filson (ed). *Trial of Frederick Bywaters and Edith Thompson*. Edinburgh: W. Hodge, 1923.

"Let Him Have It"- The Tragedy of Derek Bentley

Selwyn, Francis. *Gangland: The Case of Bentley and Craig*. London: Routledge, 1988.

Yallop, David A. *To Encourage the Others*. London: W.H. Allen, 1971.

http://www.bailii.org/ew/cases/EWCA/Crim/1998/2516.html (Transcript of the 1998 Court of Appeal proceedings)

Printed in Great Britain
by Amazon